Alcohol Use and Abuse

Perspectives on Physical Health

by Bonnie Graves

Consultant:
Patrick B. Johnson
Deputy Director, Medical Research Division
The National Center on Addiction and
Substance Abuse at Columbia University

LifeMatters
an imprint of Capstone Press
Mankato, Minnesota

LifeMatters Books are published by Capstone Press
PO Box 669 • 151 Good Counsel Drive • Mankato, Minnesota 56002
http://www.capstone-press.com

Printed in the United States of America

Library of Congress Cataloging-in-Publication Data
Graves, Bonnie B.
     Alcohol use and abuse / by Bonnie Graves.
          p.   cm.—(Perspectives on physical health)
     Includes bibliographical references and index.
     Summary: Presents information about alcohol and why it is used and abused, especially by teenagers. Also provides sources of help for alcohol-related problems.
     ISBN 0-7368-0415-3 (book)—ISBN 0-7368-0438-2 (series)
     1. Alcoholism—Juvenile literature. 2. Teenagers—Alcohol use—Juvenile literature. 3. Alcoholism—Prevention—Juvenile literature. [1. Alcoholism.] I. Title. II. Series.
     HV5066 .G72 2000
     616.86´1—dc21
                                                   99-048465
                                                 CIP

Staff Credits
Rebecca Aldridge, editor; Adam Lazar, designer; Mary Donnelly, photo researcher

Photo Credits
Cover: PNI/©StockByte
International Stock/©Stockman, 6; ©Giovanni Lunardi, 25; ©Michael Paras, 51; ©Mitch Diamond, 59
©James L. Shaffer, 48, 56
Photo Network/©Joe Outland, 15; ©Myrleen Cate, 21; ©D. & I. MacDonald, 42
PNI/©StockByte, 22
Transparencies Inc./©Billy E. Barnes, 16; ©J. Faircloth, 31
Unicorn Stock Photos/©Dennis Thompson, 12; ©Aneal Vohra, 26; ©Eric R. Berndt, 32, 37, 40; ©Jean Higgins, 35; ©Mindy Murray, 55
Visuals Unlimited/©Jeff Greenberg, 9, 47

A 09 8 7 6 5 4 3 2 1

Table of Contents

Chapter
Overview

More people are addicted to alcohol than to any other drug.

Alcohol abuse affects everyone, not just the drinker.

Most alcoholic drinks contain about ½ ounce of ethyl alcohol.

Alcohol is a depressant and a poison.

Alcohol abusers put themselves and others at risk. They have impaired judgment and exaggerated emotions.

Chapter 1

The Lowdown on Alcohol

CODY AND STEFAN, AGES 15 AND 17

Cody heard Stefan stumble into the room they shared. Cody was in bed, but he wasn't asleep. He'd been lying awake for hours waiting for his brother. Every night was the same. Stefan would leave the house sober. He would come home drunk.

The Staggering Facts

Stefan is one of the 14 million Americans who is a problem drinker. More than 3 million of these people are between ages 12 and 26. Stefan abuses alcohol, the most commonly abused drug in the United States. Each year, alcohol claims more than 100,000 lives.

Alcohol abusers are not the only people affected. The abuser's family and friends suffer as well. One in four families reports a problem with alcohol. Medical costs, time lost from work, higher insurance costs, and lower work productivity due to alcohol abuse affect everyone. The total cost to the economy is about $150 billion a year.

What's in a Drink?

Many different drinks contain alcohol. Alcohol is a chemical called ethanol, or ethyl alcohol. It is what causes a person to become intoxicated, or drunk. The three main kinds of alcoholic drinks are beer, wine, and liquor.

Every drink, no matter what kind it is, has about the same amount of alcohol. The difference is that some drinks contain more water than others do. For example, a 12-ounce beer has about ½ ounce of alcohol. A 5-ounce glass of wine has about ½ ounce of alcohol. Wine coolers and mixed drinks also contain about ½ ounce of alcohol. That means drinking four beers can get a person as drunk as four mixed drinks.

Eighty percent of teens don't know that a twelve-ounce
can of beer has the same amount of alcohol as a shot
of whiskey.

FAST FACT

Alcohol Is a Drug and a Poison

Alcohol is a drug. That means it affects how the body functions.
When alcohol is consumed, it affects all the organs and tissues
of the body. After it is swallowed, alcohol goes to the stomach
and small intestines. There it is absorbed into the bloodstream
where it is pumped to the brain and other parts of the body.
Most of the alcohol a person drinks heads straight for the small
intestine. It passes through an opening called the pyloric valve.
When a person drinks too much too fast, it can cause the valve
to swell and close. This causes the person to vomit, or throw up.

The body takes about an hour to metabolize ⅓ to ½ ounce of
alcohol. Metabolize means to break down and get rid of the
alcohol in the body. The liver does most of this breaking down.
It converts alcohol into water and carbon dioxide. Sweating and
breathing also help to break down and use up the alcohol.
Urinating, or passing liquid waste from the body, helps, too.

Alcohol affects every part of a person including mood, speech,
and coordination. The liver needs about an hour to metabolize
the alcohol in one drink. If a person drinks more than ⅓ ounce
of alcohol in an hour, he or she is going to feel its effects. One
of these effects is the slowdown of the brain and the nervous
system. As a result, a person cannot think or act as quickly. This
happens because alcohol is a depressant. Another effect is that
vision can become distorted, and a person may not see things
clearly. Also, a person's balance and judgment are off.

MYTH VS. FACT

Myth: Drinking coffee or taking a shower can help sober up someone who is drunk.

Fact: Time is the only thing that can get rid of alcohol and its effects. The liver needs time to break down the alcohol. Nothing else works.

> Jack drank several beers at a friend's party held the weekend before graduation. After the party, Jack and a group of friends chugged mixtures of rum and vodka. By the time he passed out, Jack had downed 24 drinks. His blood-alcohol level was six times the legal limit. Jack died of alcohol poisoning.
>
> **JACK, AGE 18**

Alcohol also is a poison. If too much alcohol enters a person's body too quickly, it can kill the person. Mixing alcohol with other drugs can be deadly, too. Alcohol and drugs increase the effects of each other when taken together. Alcohol also can increase the negative side effects of medication a person may be taking. Another thing alcohol does is destroy brain cells. Over time, alcohol can kill a person by gradually shutting down brain functions.

> "I don't think you should drive," Jocelyn told Taki. "You've had one too many."
>
> **TAKI, AGE 16**
>
> "I'm fine. Besides, your house is only a few blocks from here. Go on. Get in," Taki said.
>
> While driving, Taki made two wrong turns. She ended up on the highway instead of Jocelyn's street.

The Dangers of Alcohol

Drinking alcohol can put people in danger. Many people who are intoxicated don't realize that they are drunk. This is one of the most dangerous short-term effects of alcohol. It impairs judgment. Taki didn't realize she was drunk. She wasn't aware that she couldn't see or think well or react quickly. That put Taki, Jocelyn, and other people on the road in great danger. About 25,000 people in the United States die each year because of drunk drivers.

Drinking causes other problems, too. People who are intoxicated can't think clearly. They may have extreme emotions. Problem drinking increases the risk of violent behavior and abuse. For example, three out of five cases of child abuse occur after drinking.

Points to Consider

Why do you think people abuse alcohol?

Which of the facts about alcohol abuse is the most staggering to you? Why?

Why do you think that more people are addicted to alcohol than to any other drug?

People have been making and drinking alcohol for 10,000 years. Nearly every culture has used and misused alcohol.

In the United States, alcohol has had a long and mixed history. The government tried unsuccessfully to ban alcohol with the 18th Amendment.

Teens drink for many reasons, including peer pressure, advertising influences, and wanting alcohol's effects.

The rate of teen drinking declined between 1979 and 1996.

Chapter **2**
Why Do People Drink?

History of Alcohol

Animals were probably the first to discover alcohol. Most likely, the discovery happened by accident. You see, alcohol is made naturally during a process called fermentation. During this process, yeast spores, or cells, in fruits, vegetables, or grains convert sugar into alcohol and carbon dioxide. So some unsuspecting bird could have dined on fermented berries long ago. That bird might have been the first to experience the intoxicating effects of ethyl alcohol.

Humans discovered alcohol thousands of years ago. Probably their first discovery was by accident, too. Since then, alcohol has become humankind's most popular drug. It has been used for at least 10,000 years.

Almost every culture has found a way to produce alcohol. Some people use fruit such as grapes to make wine. Others use grains such as barley or rice to make beer. Another drink was invented in the 8th century. It was made by boiling fermented grains or fruit. The vapor was captured and then cooled. When the vapor cooled, it returned to liquid form. The result was a liquid that had a strong taste and a high alcohol content. This liquid is known as liquor. The process by which liquor is made is called distillation.

History of Use and Misuse of Alcohol

Through the centuries, alcohol has been used and misused by almost all cultures. In the city of Babylon, 4,000 years ago, alcohol abuse was condemned because of the problems it caused. The Bible mentions the use of wine and its dangers. Muslim followers in the 7th century forbade the use of alcohol altogether.

Alcohol Use and Abuse

Types of drinkers:

Light = Fewer than three drinks per week

Moderate = Fewer than two drinks per day

Heavy = Two to four drinks per day or five drinks at a time at least five times per month

Very heavy = More than four drinks per day

Binge = Four to five drinks during a short period of time

Alcohol has had a long and mixed history in the United States. The early settlers drank beer and wine. Puritans in the 17th century also drank. However, they considered drunkenness a crime. They called for moderation in drinking but not abstinence, or complete avoidance.

As the country grew, more and more people consumed alcohol. The ill effects of alcohol became apparent. By 1855, 13 states had laws prohibiting the use of alcohol. In 1919, the 18th Amendment, or the National Prohibition Act, went into effect. This act made it illegal to make, sell, or buy alcoholic drinks. Congress passed the 21st Amendment 14 years later. This amendment put an end to Prohibition.

"I started drinking to deal with school and problems. I began in the morning. I kept drinking all day. If I didn't drink, I got a headache and felt like I was going to throw up."—Terry, age 17

"I drink because most of the crowd I hang out with drinks. Mostly I drink wine coolers. I don't like the taste of beer or wine."—Leon, age 16

Travis popped the champagne cork. He started pouring the bubbly liquid into everyone's glass. Travis walked up to his sister, Evie. She was just 14, a junior bridesmaid. Travis winked at her and filled her glass, too. "Lift your glasses high, folks," Travis said. "It's time to toast the bride and groom."

EVIE, AGE 14

Drinking Today

Today, as in the past, alcohol plays a role in our culture. Alcohol is served almost everywhere. It is poured at parties, picnics, and weddings. It is used to toast and to christen, or dedicate. Some people use it to unwind. However, alcohol also is misused and abused.

Alcohol abuse, or the harmful use of alcohol, can happen to anyone. People of any race whether young, old, rich, poor, men, or women all are subject to it. Studies have shown some differences in risk for alcohol abuse. For example, men are more likely than women to abuse alcohol.

AYITA, AGE 17

"Hey, Rafael's having a party Friday night. Want to go?" Paul asked.

"Will there be drinking?" Ayita asked.

"Yeah, probably," Paul said.

"Then forget it," Ayita told him.

"Don't be a drag, Ayita," Paul said. "Everybody drinks. What's the big deal?"

The Attraction of Teens to Drinking

Why do some teens choose to drink while others do not? You probably know some of the reasons. Some teens drink to fit in. They may think, "My friends do it, so why shouldn't I?" They may believe that drinking is a way to feel mature and to have fun. Many teens drink hoping to find relief from boredom, loneliness, anger, unhappiness, or pressure.

Some teens may drink because the adults in their life do. These teens may be living in a home where alcohol is served. Perhaps they think drinking is the norm. Other teens might come from a home in which alcohol is forbidden. Teens from these homes may drink to rebel.

Advertisements also may play a role in teen drinking. Ads for beer or wine coolers often show attractive people having a good time. The message is "Drink our beer, and you will be attractive and have lots of friends, too."

Some teens drink because they may expect alcohol to make them feel a certain way. They may expect alcohol to relax them. Teens may think they will feel less self-conscious when they drink. They may expect that drinking will make them more fun to be with. The problem is many teens don't know the risks of drinking. They don't know what alcohol can do to their body and their brain.

Currently, 1.9 million young people between the ages of 12 and 20 are heavy drinkers. That means they consume five alcoholic drinks at a time at least five times a month. Or it can mean they drink two to four alcoholic drinks every day. Nearly 4.5 million teens are binge drinkers. That means they drink four to five drinks in a short period of time.

Fifty-six percent of students in grades five through twelve said that alcohol ads encouraged them to drink.

The Good News

Teens are becoming more aware of the risks associated with alcohol. In the last 20 years, more and more teens have said "no" to alcohol. In 1979, nearly 50 percent of kids between ages 12 and 17 regularly used alcohol. By 1996, this percentage had dropped to less than 20 percent. The percentage of nondrinking adults is increasing as well. Today, more than two out of five American adults do not drink.

Points to Consider

Have you ever been around someone who has had too much to drink? How did that person act? How did that person's actions make you feel?

Why do you think some teens drink even though it is illegal?

What do you think are some reasons for the decline in teen drinking between 1979 and 1996?

Chapter Overview

Alcoholics are people who are addicted to alcohol. They crave alcohol and cannot control their drinking. They have a physical dependence on alcohol. Also, their alcohol tolerance increases with time.

Alcoholism is a disease that develops over time. It can be treated but not cured.

Heredity, environment, and a person's psychological makeup all play a role in alcoholism.

Many signs indicate that someone might be an alcoholic.

Some people abuse alcohol but are not alcoholics. They are not addicted to alcohol, but they have the same problems alcoholics do. A binge drinker is a type of alcohol abuser.

Chapter **3**

The Difference Between Alcoholics and Alcohol Abusers

What Is an Alcoholic?

An alcoholic is someone who is addicted to alcohol. That means he or she can't get along either physically or emotionally without alcohol. For alcoholics, alcohol becomes their main resource for dealing with people, work, and life. It rules their thoughts, emotions, and actions.

Studies show about 9.3 percent of men and 1.9
percent of women are heavy drinkers. The heaviest
drinkers are men ages 18 to 29. Men also experience
more of the adverse, or negative, effects of alcohol
than women do.

"Do your parents drink?" Luke asked Rana and Denzel.

LUKE, AGE 15

"Sure," Rana said. "Mine have wine with dinner sometimes."

"Yeah, mine too," Denzel said. "Every weekend my dad has a drink or two before dinner. Then he drinks wine during and after dinner."

"Does he stop? Or does he just keep on drinking?" Luke asked.

"I usually don't stick around long enough to find out. Sometimes he gets pretty nasty with my mom. Why do you ask?" Denzel replied.

Luke didn't say anything. Rana knew by the look on Luke's face that something was wrong. "My mom drinks every night. She just keeps drinking until she passes out on the couch," Luke finally said.

Most people who drink, such as Rana's parents, can limit the amount. They can stay in control. Other people, such as Luke's mom and Denzel's dad, aren't as lucky. Denzel's dad is an alcohol abuser. Luke's mom is an alcoholic.

The National Institute on Alcohol Abuse and Alcoholism (NIAAA) says that there are four distinguishing characteristics of an alcoholic. These characteristics are craving, impaired control, physical dependence, and tolerance.

Alcoholics develop a craving for alcohol. They become obsessed with the idea of having a drink.

Once alcoholics start drinking, they can't stop. They have no built-in signal to tell them it's time to quit.

An alcoholic's body gets hooked on the effects of alcohol. When the person doesn't get alcohol, his or her body misses these effects. The alcoholic goes through withdrawal. Some symptoms, or evidence, of withdrawal include extreme anxiety, shaking, and seizures.

Alcoholics develop a tolerance for alcohol. That means alcoholics must drink more and more to experience the same effects.

Alcohol addiction is a disease that develops over time. It can take months or even years. Alcoholism can't be cured, but it can be treated. More than 1.5 million Americans are currently in recovery from alcoholism.

Lori started drinking in high school. She thought it was no big LORI, AGE 19 deal. Sometimes she got drunk at parties. She believed she could take alcohol or leave it. Then Lori met Mark. He was 21. Lori was 18. Mark could buy liquor, and he did. Mark and Lori drank every weekend and sometimes during the week.

Lori soon realized she had to drink more and more to get the same "buzz." By the time Mark broke up with Lori a year later, Lori was drinking all the time. If she didn't drink, she would feel shaky and queasy, or like she had to throw up. Lori didn't start out an alcoholic. She became one.

How Does a Person Become an Alcoholic?

No simple answers explain why a person becomes an alcoholic. However, one thing is certain. No one can become an alcoholic without drinking. Also, no one can become an alcoholic overnight. How much a person drinks and how often both play a role in alcoholism. However, alcohol alone doesn't cause alcoholism. If it did, anyone who took a drink would become addicted.

Children of alcoholics are three to four times more likely to become alcoholics than children of nonalcoholics are.

Most researchers believe that at least three factors are involved in alcoholism. These factors are heredity, environment, and psychological, or mental, makeup. Studies have shown that heredity plays a role in alcoholism. Genes, or important parts of cells, from parents may make some people more likely than others to become alcoholic. However, most children of alcoholics do not become alcoholics themselves.

Environment also plays a role in alcoholism. Social factors including family, friends, and advertisements can influence drinking behavior.

Psychological traits are the third factor in alcoholism. A person's attitudes and personality can contribute to drinking patterns. For example, some teens are impulsive or thrill-seeking. These teens may be more likely than others to become problem drinkers. Severely depressed or anxious people also are at high risk for alcoholism.

To prevent alcoholism a person needs to:

Understand the disease and be aware of its symptoms

Know that alcohol is a drug and that its use includes potential risks

Avoid high-risk drinking

Know his or her family's history with alcohol

Be familiar with sources of help

Warning Signs of Alcoholism

During the development of alcoholism, certain signs appear. These signs are:

Excessive drinking or frequent drunkenness

Increased tolerance to alcohol

Blackouts, or not remembering what happened

Shaking

Job loss

Feeling the need for a drink; that something is missing if one doesn't drink

Inability to pace drinking as well as gulping drinks

Use of alcohol to relieve tension

Interference with family life

Denial of the negative effects of alcohol

What Is an Alcohol Abuser?

Unlike alcoholics, alcohol abusers are not addicted to alcohol. However, they do drink too much. They may drink frequently. You don't have to be an alcoholic to have a drinking problem. However, people who abuse alcohol are more likely to become alcoholics than people who do not abuse alcohol.

People who abuse alcohol have many of the same problems as alcoholics. However, they do not experience these problems to the same degree or as frequently as alcoholics do. Some of these problems are discussed in the next chapters.

College was my first time away from home. I didn't drink in high CARL, AGE 20 school, but that soon changed once I got to college. Everyone drank there. On weekends, I'd party with my friends. We'd go from one party or bar to the next. At each place I'd drink at least two beers, maybe three. Every weekend, I'd get wasted. I'd barf or pass out or both.

Carl is a type of alcohol abuser called a binge drinker. He didn't drink to be social. He didn't drink for fun. He drank to get wasted. Binge drinking is a problem in high schools and colleges.

Binge drinkers consume four or five alcoholic drinks in a short time span. These people put themselves in danger. Their body can't handle that much alcohol. Also, they may pass out and vomit. This puts them in danger of suffocating from their own vomit. Binge drinkers also affect the people around them. This is because binge drinkers often have a lack of respect for the rights of others.

Alcohol Use and Abuse

"Binge drinking is not cool at all. I want people to respect me. I also want to stay healthy and have a long life. Not bingeing helps me in both of those areas."
—Renato, age 16

Points to Consider

Have you seen signs that someone you know is abusing alcohol? Explain.

Many factors can cause someone to become an alcoholic. Which factor do you think is most important and why?

How would you describe the difference between someone who abuses alcohol and an alcoholic?

What is binge drinking? Why is it dangerous?

People who drink alcohol may lose the respect of their friends. They also may lose self-control and self-respect.

Drinking too much alcohol can cost a person his or her health.

Drinking alcohol increases a person's chances for accidents and puts other people at risk.

Alcohol abuse comes at a high price for the abuser and the people in the abuser's life.

Chapter **4**

The Price of Drinking

The cost of drinking is not calculated just in dollar amounts. Drinking increases the chance for many sorts of bad things to happen. This risk increases not just for the drinker but for everyone in the drinker's life as well.

There may be consequences whenever a person drinks alcohol because it is a drug. A person's body and brain are affected first. Then actions are affected. Often these actions can harm the drinker. They may harm other people, too. The more alcohol a person consumes, the greater the risk. The longer a person consumes alcohol, the greater the risk. However, some risk is involved even after having only one drink.

Almost half of college students who were victims of campus crimes said they had been drinking or using other drugs.

Tanya, Age 17

Tanya was an honor student. She was quiet, but people respected her. Her friends could count on her. During her senior year, Tanya decided to change her image. At a Halloween party, Tanya took her first drink. It loosened her up. She started telling jokes. People laughed. Tanya felt funny and liked. Tanya took a second drink and a third. Her jokes started getting nastier and louder. People stopped laughing, but Tanya didn't notice. After Tanya had her fourth drink, she staggered out the door. She fell over and started throwing up.

Losing Your Cool

There's nothing cool about being loud and obnoxious, or annoying. Normally, Tanya wasn't either one. However, alcohol affects a person's brain. It causes unclear thinking and impaired judgment. Drinking alcohol made Tanya careless with her remarks and actions. Barfing certainly didn't win her respect, either.

Jeff and his friends had booked a hotel room for prom night. It seemed like a terrific idea because after prom they could drink, and no one would have to drive.

Prom night finally arrived. Jeff thought Mara looked sexy. All during the dance Jeff kept thinking about the hotel room.

At last, the prom was over. Jeff, Mara, and three other couples drove to the hotel. They started drinking. Before Jeff knew it, he and Mara were on the bed. The next thing he remembered was Mara screaming, "You tried to rape me!"

Losing Self-Control and Self-Respect

Alcohol tends to make people less inhibited, or restrained. Researchers are not certain why this happens. It may be a chemical effect of alcohol. It may result from a drinker's expectation of how the drug will affect him or her. Regardless, people who drink may feel less self-restrained. For example, alcohol can turn a normal sex drive into overdrive.

Instead of a night to remember, Jeff and Mara's prom date turned into a nightmare. It could have been worse, though. Jeff and Mara could have had unprotected sex. They could have put themselves at risk for sexually transmitted diseases (STDs). These are diseases passed through sexual contact. Alcohol also can cause temporary impotence, or inability to engage in sexual intercourse. Jeff and Mara also lost their self-respect because of alcohol.

FAYE, AGE 15

Faye started drinking after her parents got divorced. She didn't drink much at first. Then things got out of hand. She started drinking every day. Faye got into fights with her mom. Soon she started fighting with her friends, too. Before Faye knew it, all her old friends were gone. The only people she had to hang out with were other kids who drank. Even Faye admitted most of them were losers.

Losing Your Friends

Teens may fear losing friends if they do not join others in drinking. However, people who drink too much alcohol are the ones at risk of losing their friends.

Alcohol drains the body of vitamins and minerals. This can hurt your immune system. A weakened immune system means you get sick more often.

Alcoholics and alcohol abusers can be difficult to be around. Alcohol makes them edgy. Sometimes just about anything can cause them to fly off the handle. People who have problems with alcohol also may start to sneak around to hide their habit. They may lie to cover up what they are doing. These behaviors are hard on the people in the drinker's life. Drinking can cause major strain on family members. It can cause friends to disappear. The drinker's companions may be only other drinkers.

Losing Your Health

Drinking alcohol makes it hard for a person to function at his or her best. In the short term, drinking can make a person feel dizzy. It also can make a person feel nauseous, or like he or she is going to throw up. It can cause sweating and restlessness. It lowers body temperature and can make a person feel shaky.

Over time, drinking can cause major health problems. These problems include a liver disease called cirrhosis and several kinds of cancer. Drinking also increases the risk of heart disease. Heavy use of alcohol can damage nearly every body organ and system.

Alcoholism is the third biggest killer in the United States. It ranks only behind heart disease and cancer.

Losing Life and Limb

Alcohol not only impairs judgment and coordination, but also it lengthens reaction time. That means it takes longer for the body to respond. This makes drinkers prime candidates for accidents. Alcohol-related car accidents kill thousands of children and teens each year. Other alcohol-related accidents include falling and drowning. People who consume alcohol are more likely to be fire or burn victims. They also are more likely to be victims of crime.

An overdose of alcohol can kill. An overdose is taking too much of a drug. Alcohol overdoses cause more deaths among children and teens than do overdoses of any other drug. Overdosing is a special danger for teens because many of them aren't aware of alcohol's effects. Teens may want to impress their peers with their drinking ability. However, many teens don't know that too much alcohol can kill them.

Drinking too much alcohol also shortens a person's life. Consuming two or more alcoholic drinks a day can increase the risk of death by 50 percent. On average, an alcoholic lives 10 to 12 fewer years than a nonalcoholic.

Putting Others at Risk

Each year drunk drivers kill thousands of innocent people. In the United States, about 50,000 people die in car accidents each year. Almost 25,000 of those deaths are alcohol-related. The risk of having a fatal accident goes up even after one drink.

In addition to impairing vision and reaction time, alcohol impairs moral judgment. It also reduces inhibition, or self-control, and increases aggression. This makes the alcohol abuser ripe for abusive behavior that may lead to violence. Half of all homicides, or killings, involve alcohol.

Women who drink alcohol can harm their unborn babies, too. Their babies are at risk for alcohol-related birth defects. The name for this problem is fetal alcohol syndrome (FAS). Babies born with FAS have many types of physical, mental, and emotional problems.

ADVICE FROM TEENS

What should you do if the driver for your ride home has been drinking?

"Try to get the driver to hand over the keys."
—Lisa, age 15

"Call your parents or take a cab."—Vince, age 14

"Call a friend!"—Pablo, age 17

"Don't get into the car. Period."—Nandi, age 18

Everyone Loses

Everyone loses when it comes to alcohol abuse. Drinkers lose their self-respect and relationships. They lose their health and sometimes their lives. Nonabusers also lose. Innocent people are killed or have loved ones who are killed because of alcohol abuse. Friends and family members suffer. Even unborn babies are put at risk.

Points to Consider

Imagine that you are the ruler of a country. Seventy percent of your people drink socially. Ten percent don't drink at all. Twenty percent abuse alcohol. Every year you spend about $2 billion to repair the lives and property ruined by alcohol. Would you ban alcoholic drinks in your country? Why or why not?

What does it mean to have self-respect? Do you think a person who drinks too much has self-respect? Why or why not?

How would you feel if your best friend started abusing alcohol? Why do you think you would feel this way?

In what ways do alcohol abusers put other people at risk?

Knowing that pressures to drink exist can help a person to resist them.

To drink means to risk out-of-control behavior that can be costly in many different ways.

Not drinking has many benefits.

For some adults, moderate drinking can be beneficial. However, for teens, drinking is both illegal and risky.

Chapter 5

To Drink or Not to Drink?

In North America today, it is hard to avoid alcohol. Most towns have their share of places to buy or drink alcohol. Some teens may see parents or friends drink. Some teens may not know anyone who drinks. However, television or movies probably expose them to people drinking.

Rachel drove down Main Street. Everywhere she looked she saw

RACHEL, AGE 16

evidence of liquor. Signs for beer hung in the deli window. Two men sat at a sidewalk cafe sipping wine. A neon cocktail glass flashed above the entrance to Toby's restaurant. By the time Rachel reached the end of town, she had lost count of all the signs of alcohol.

Her health teacher, Mr. Batz, was right. Alcohol is everywhere.

The Pressure to Drink

Some teens may feel pressured to drink. Others may not. Regardless, the pressures are out there. Teens who know about these pressures are better prepared not to fall into their traps. Curiosity is one trap. Other traps include boredom, loneliness, stress, or depression. Alcohol cannot relieve any of these feelings. In fact, in the long run, alcohol does just the opposite. It makes people more lonely, more stressed out, and more depressed. Alcohol sometimes plays a role in suicide. In fact, alcohol is involved one out of every four times that someone takes his or her own life.

Alcohol Use and Abuse

"The kids I know don't really enjoy drinking. But it's a status thing at my school. It's cool to say, 'I got drunk last night.' I'd say about a third of the seniors get drunk at parties weekly."—Ben, age 18

Friends and peers may cause pressure, too. This is an area that is being carefully studied. Everyone wants to fit in and be liked. Teens may feel the pressure to drink just to fit in with their friends.

Ads for alcoholic drinks can be another pressure. Many of the ads make drinking look fun and mature. They show good-looking people having a great time. Many teens are in a hurry to mature. And who doesn't want to look good and have fun? Without even thinking about it consciously, teens may link having friends and good times with drinking. The alcohol industry spends $2 billion each year on this kind of subtle pressure.

Risks of Drinking

People who drink risk out-of-control behavior. This could cause a person to:

Become abusive or violent; possible consequences include jail time, injuries, or death.

Act irresponsibly regarding sex; possible consequences include pregnancy or STDs such as AIDS.

Break the law; possible consequences include jail time, injuries, or death.

Drive, swim, or bicycle while drunk; possible consequences include jail time, injuries, or death.

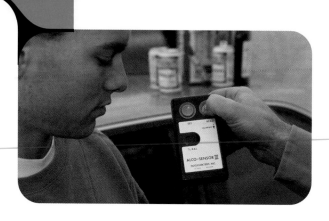

In addition to risky behavior, drinking puts the mind and body at risk. Some of these risks are:

Increased loneliness and depression that can lead to suicide

Acute alcohol poisoning that causes hangovers, or sickness, and sometimes death

Addiction

Overdosing or taking other drugs; possible consequences include coma, paralysis, or death.

Poor athletic performance

Liver or heart disease or cancer

Interference with grades and friendships

Benefits of Not Drinking

Teens who choose not to drink usually look and feel good. They don't have hangovers. They do not risk letting their grades slide. Teens who are involved in sports perform better without alcohol in their body. Not drinking lessens the chance of getting liver or heart disease or cancer. It adds 10 to 12 years to a person's life. People who do not drink are in control and do not put others at risk.

Is Some Drinking Okay?

Studies have shown that for adults a small amount of drinking can be beneficial. It can reduce the risk of heart attacks. It can help lower cholesterol and prevent colds. For teens, however, drinking is not beneficial. In the United States, drinking is illegal until age 21. There are good reasons why. Drinking can interfere with a teen's normal development. Teens need time to learn life skills and ways of coping. Drinking can cut that time short.

Points to Consider

What are some of the reasons teens drink? Do you think any of them are good ones? Why or why not?

What are some of the risks of losing control because of drinking?

What do you think is the greatest benefit of not drinking? Explain.

Denial is one of the symptoms of alcoholism. It is the biggest roadblock in helping the problem drinker.

Alcohol abuse and alcoholism can be treated. In some cases, the alcoholic needs to be hospitalized.

Counseling and support groups are part of the recovery program for alcohol abusers and alcoholics.

Several methods exist for treating alcoholics and alcohol abusers, but their goals are the same. These goals are to get and keep the person sober.

Alcoholism is a family affair. Any successful treatment includes the family as well as the alcoholic.

Chapter **6**

Quitting

"Get off my back. I'm no alcoholic. I drink a few beers. So what? I can stop if I want to," Scott said.

SCOTT, AGE 17

"I think you drink more than a few beers, Scott. I think you need help. I wish you'd talk to someone," Rudy said.

"My doctor and my counselor told me patience was one key to getting well. My alcoholism didn't happen overnight. Things weren't going to get better at lightning speed, either. Things were going to take time.

"Another key was a willingness to recover. It may take more than one try. That's no reason to give up. Getting well is hard work. But with time, patience, and support, it can be done.

"My doctor and my counselor were right. I haven't had a drink in a year. I have a good job and a boyfriend who treats me with respect."
—Cindy, a recovering alcoholic

Admitting a Problem Exists

Maybe you know an alcohol abuser or an alcoholic. Maybe you are one yourself. The most difficult thing for a drinker to do is to admit that a problem exists. Denial is one of the symptoms of alcoholism and alcohol abuse. It prevents the abuser from getting help. Asking tough questions may help reveal the truth. The following questions are from the National Council on Alcoholism and Drug Dependence (NCADD):

Do you use alcohol to build self-confidence?

Do you ever drink right after you have a problem at home or school?

Have you missed school because of alcohol?

Does it bother you if someone says that you use too much alcohol?

Have you started hanging out with a heavy-drinking crowd?

Do you feel bummed out after using alcohol?

Have you gotten into trouble for using alcohol?

Have you lost friends since you started using alcohol?

Do you drink until all your supply is gone?

Do you ever wake up and wonder what happened the night before?

Do you think you have a problem with alcohol?

Answering yes to any three of the previous questions indicates a risk for developing alcoholism. Answering yes to five questions indicates immediate professional help is needed.

Jay sat with his mom in his pastor's office. He was nervous.

JAY, AGE 15

He was there because the youth director had blown the whistle on him.

"Bayview Hospital has an excellent program for alcoholics," Pastor Flynn said.

"An alcoholic? Me?" Jay thought. "What is Pastor Flynn thinking? Maybe I drink, but I'm no alcoholic. Pastor Flynn is so wrong! Why is he babbling on about treatment programs?"

Getting Help

Plenty of help is available for alcohol abusers and alcoholics. School counselors, doctors, or staff at health clinics can recommend medical help. They also can suggest others who can help the drinker deal with social and psychological problems.

Medical professionals can help with problems of withdrawal. People with mild to moderate symptoms can be treated as outpatients. That means they don't have to go into a hospital. These people can get help for withdrawal from their doctor at his or her office. A doctor also can assign counseling and suggest support groups.

A hospital or treatment center is recommended for people with severe withdrawal symptoms. At these places, people get a physical and psychological exam. Then they go through detoxification, or a process of ridding the alcohol from their body. The detox period takes from three to seven days.

Disulfiram, commonly called Antabuse®, is a drug sometimes prescribed to curb drinking. Antabuse makes the person taking it physically ill if he or she drinks alcohol.

People also can be treated with psychotherapy that deals with mental and emotional problems or with behavioral therapy. They may be introduced to Alcoholics Anonymous (AA), a program designed to help alcohol abusers and alcoholics. This program is free and offers help for staying sober one day at a time. The AA program is based on 12 steps. The first of these steps is for the abuser to admit that he or she has no power over alcohol. The AA program has been highly successful. Most countries today have AA groups.

No two alcoholics are alike. There is no best method for treating the disease, either. Whatever the treatment, the goals are the same. One goal is to help the alcoholic get sober. Another goal is to help the alcoholic learn the skills needed to stay sober. The following are six steps to recovery:

Admit a drinking problem exists.

Get and stay sober one day at a time.

Accept the support of others.

Develop nondrinking friendships and interests.

Develop the coping skills needed for dealing with work or school and relationships.

Have self-respect and look forward to each day with eagerness and confidence.

Marty Mann was the first woman to get sober through Alcoholics Anonymous (AA). She founded the National Council on Alcoholism and Drug Dependence in 1944. She helped people understand that alcoholism is a disease that is preventable and treatable.

"Terry, this week it's your turn to have the meeting at your house," Addie said.

TERRY, AGE 18

Terry got a horrible feeling in the pit of her stomach. She couldn't have the meeting at her house. She couldn't chance it. She never knew what her dad would do. Well, that wasn't quite true. She knew he would drink. She just didn't know how he would act. If he yelled at her or her friends, she just couldn't bear it.

What Family and Friends Can Do

Effective alcohol treatment programs include family counseling because family members need appropriate help to recover as well. Al-Anon and Alateen are two organizations that can help. These are organizations for friends and family members of alcoholics. Their numbers are listed at the back of this book.

If someone in your life abuses alcohol, you are not alone. About 11 million children and teens in the United States have an alcoholic parent. What you need to remember is that your parent is not a bad person. He or she has a disease. It's a disease that makes people lose control when drinking. You can't control or stop your parent's drinking. Also remember, you are not the reason your parent drinks.

The Columbia University College of Physicians and Surgeons has these suggestions for families and friends of alcoholics:

Realize that the alcoholic will never be able to drink safely.

Accept that the alcoholic is sick and cannot control drinking.

Stop rescuing the alcoholic from his or her mistakes.

Seek information about alcoholism. Know that it is a treatable disease with a good recovery rate.

Family and friends alone can't give the help an alcoholic needs. The person needs the help of people trained to treat the disease. The sources at the back of this book can lead you to people who can help.

Points to Consider

Why do you think it is so hard for an alcoholic or alcohol abuser to admit a problem exists?

What are two goals of any alcohol treatment program?

Why is it important for an alcoholic to develop nondrinking friendships and interests?

Why do family members need to be involved in an alcoholic's recovery?

Alcohol abuse can be prevented by knowing the facts and by making wise choices.

You can help a friend with a drinking problem by voicing your concern and being a good listener. You can offer to help, to get information, and to get help for yourself.

If you think you have a drinking problem, you can learn the facts about alcohol. You also can accept that you have a problem and take action.

There are two good ways to keep from drinking. These ways include learning the facts about alcohol and being prepared to say no.

One good way to keep friends from drinking is not to drink yourself.

Chapter **7**

What You Can Do

"Okay, we've finished our unit on alcohol abuse. Who has an idea on how to prevent it?" Mr. Donnelly asked.

ASABI, AGE 14

"With the facts," Asabi said. "If kids knew the facts, they could make wiser choices. What if we put on a skit for the fifth and sixth graders? We could do one on the risks of drinking."

Alcohol abuse can be prevented. It helps to know the facts. The sooner a person knows them the better. In the United States, people are usually age 12 or 13 when they first try alcohol.

> I thought Kari just drank at parties. She drank a lot but never got drunk. Then she started coming to school late. I could smell booze on her breath. That's when I started to worry.
>
> **CHULA, AGE 15**

If You Suspect a Friend Has a Drinking Problem

If you suspect a friend has a drinking problem, don't nag or preach to that person. That won't do anything but irritate him or her. It's best to voice your concern when your friend isn't under the influence of alcohol. That is when you should tell him or her what you have noticed and why you're worried.

You also should be willing to listen and to offer help. This could mean going to an AA meeting with your friend. It could mean getting information or talking to a counselor. You could offer to get information from the sources listed at the back of this book.

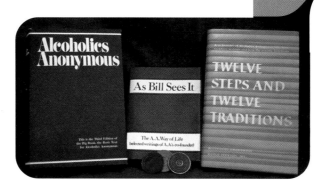

Often, a friend abusing alcohol doesn't want help. It is hard to help someone who does not want it. The National Council on Alcoholism and Drug Dependence (NCADD) can help in this type of situation. This organization operates a National Intervention Network that helps to plan, rehearse, and conduct an intervention. During an intervention, specially trained people meet with the alcohol abuser. The organization's number is listed at the back of this book.

It also is important to get help for yourself. You could contact Alateen. The number is listed at the back of this book. Alateen can give you tips on how to deal with your friend. You may want to talk with your school nurse or counselor. Try to get all the information you can about the disease. The more you know, the more you can help your friend.

TYRONE, AGE 17

Tyrone started out having a few beers on the weekends. Normally he was uptight at parties. Beer made him relax. He had more fun when he drank. Soon a few beers didn't do the job anymore. Sometimes at parties he would drink a whole six-pack. He was starting to wonder if maybe he had a drinking problem.

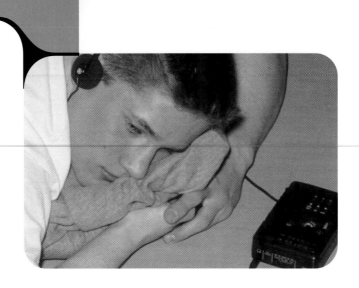

If You Drink

Maybe you suspect you have a drinking problem. You can ask yourself the questions on pages 46–47 if you want to find out. Another important step to take is to learn about the dangers of alcohol. You have already begun by reading this book, but there are many more resources to help you. Some of these are listed in the back of this book.

The hardest part of recovery is to accept that you have a problem. It is important to remember that denial is your number one enemy.

Taking action and looking for better ways to solve your problems also are important. For Tyrone, that means finding a better way to relax. He may decide to try deep breathing or listening to quiet music when he needs to relax. For you, taking action might mean trying to find another way to relieve depression. You may want to talk with a doctor, nurse, or counselor. You may want to join AA. If you seek help, you will make many people besides yourself very glad that you did.

If someone asks you if you want a drink, how do you say no?

"'No thanks.' It's simple, but it works for me!"
—Freda, age 14

"Booze makes me puke."—Sean, age 16

"I'm on a diet. Too many calories."—Wanaka, age 17

"Why is it so important to you for me to drink?"
—John, age 18

To Keep Yourself From Drinking

The best way to say no to drinking is to learn the facts. The more you know, the less you'll want to start. However, even that may not be enough. What about those pressure situations? How can you prepare for those? What if someone asks you to drink? What do you say? Here are some tips on how to say no.

1. **Give a reason.** Someone may say, "Have a drink. You'll have a better time." You could respond, "Alcohol makes me sick. I'm already having a good time."

2. **Have something else to do.** "No, thanks. I'm going to dance."

3. **Be prepared for different kinds of pressure.** If the pressure seems threatening, you might have to just walk away.

4. **Make it simple.** There's no need to explain if you don't want to. Just say, "No, thanks." If that doesn't work, just say it stronger.

Another solution is to avoid the situation. Don't go to a party if you know there's going to be drinking. What if you're not sure there will be drinking? A good idea in this case is to make up your mind in advance. Decide before the party that you are not going to drink. Then, when someone asks you, you will have an answer ready.

"Both my parents abused alcohol. What saved me was finally talking to someone about it. My advice to any kids who have an alcoholic parent is this: Find someone you trust who will talk with you. It could be a friend's parent, a teacher, or even a big sister or brother. Call them when you need to talk. It helps a lot."
—Omar, age 15

"Thanks, Elki," Maddie said.

"Thanks?" Elki asked. "For what?"

"For not drinking at Jeff's party. That really gave me the courage to say 'no.'"

MADDIE, AGE 18

To Keep Your Peers From Starting to Drink

How do you keep your peers from drinking? Being a good role model is the most effective way. If you say no to drinking, your friends probably will, too. You may want to do as many teens have done and join Students Against Destructive Decisions (SADD). One of the things SADD does is promote alcohol-free parties. SADD has chapters in every state. Addresses for SADD can be found at its Internet site listed at the back of this book.

Points to Consider

Can alcohol abuse be prevented? Explain.

If you had a friend with a drinking problem, what could you do to help?

If you have a drinking problem, what are some things you could do to help yourself?

If you don't drink, how can you keep yourself from starting?

How could you keep other teens from drinking?

Glossary

denial (di-NYE-uhl)—refusal to believe or admit that a problem exists

depressant (di-PRESS-uhnt)—a type of drug that slows down a person's mind and body

drug (DRUHG)—a substance that changes the way the brain and body work

environment (en-VYE-ruhn-muhnt)—the surroundings and conditions that affect growth and development

hangover (HANG-oh-vur)—the sick feeling someone gets after drinking too much alcohol

heredity (huh-RED-uh-tee)—passing on of certain traits from parents to children through the genes

impotence (IM-puh-tuhnss)—inability to perform sexual intercourse

intervention (in-tur-VEN-shuhn)—an action taken to change a situation

intoxication (in-tok-suh-KAYE-shuhn)—the effect of having too much alcohol in the body; drunkenness.

metabolize (muh-TAB-uh-lize)—to break down and chemically change a substance that a person eats or drinks

nauseous (NAW-shuhss)—feeling like you are going to throw up

psychological (sye-kuh-LOJ-uh-kuhl)—relating to the mind or emotions

psychotherapy (sye-ko-THER-uh-pee)—treatment for mental and emotional problems

therapy (THER-uh-pee)—any treatment meant to improve a person's health or well-being

tolerance (TOL-ur-uhnss)—the mind and body needing more and more of a drug to get the same effect

withdrawal (with-DRAW-uhl)—the period following the discontinued use of a habit-forming drug; withdrawal often is marked by uncomfortable physical and psychological symptoms.

For More Information

Landau, Elaine. *Teenage Drinking.* Springfield, NJ: Enslow Publishers, 1994.

Pringle, Laurence P. *Drinking: A Risky Business.* New York: Morrow & Co., 1997.

Ryan, Elizabeth A. *Straight Talk About Drugs and Alcohol.* New York: Facts on File, 1996.

Steins, Richard. *Alcohol Abuse: Is This Danger on the Rise?* New York: Twenty-First Century Books, 1995.

Useful Addresses and Internet Sites

Alateen

Al-Anon Family Group Headquarters

1600 Corporate Landing Parkway

Virginia Beach, VA 23454-5617

1-800-344-2666 (in the United States)

1-800-443-4525 (in Canada)

www.al-anon.alateen.org

Alcoholics Anonymous

PO Box 459

Grand Central Station

New York, NY 10163

American Council for Drug Education

(ACDE)

164 West 74th Street

New York, NY 10023

1-800-488-DRUG (800-488-3784)

www.acde.org

Canadian Centre on Substance Abuse

75 Albert Street, Suite 300

Ottawa, ON K1P 5E7

CANADA

www.ccsa.ca

National Clearinghouse for Alcohol and Drug

Information (NCADI)

PO Box 2345

Rockville, MD 20847-2345

1-800-729-6686

www.health.org

National Council on Alcoholism and Drug
Dependence, Inc. (NCADD)

12 West 21 Street

New York, NY 10010

1-800-NCA-CALL (800-622-2255)

www.ncadd.org

National Institute on Alcohol Abuse and
Alcoholism (NIAAA)

6000 Executive Boulevard—Willco Building

Bethesda, MD 20892-7003

www.niaaa.nih.gov

Do It Now Foundation

www.doitnow.org

Contains a variety of articles and publications

on alcohol and other drug use

Students Against Destructive Decisions

(SADD)

www.saddonline.com

Provides information on SADD, the

opportunity to chat with SADD members, and

stories related to problem drinking

Index

Index continued